The Mighty Oak and Me

A Mr. Pish Backyard Adventure

K. S. Brooks

and

Mr. Pish
The Traveling Terrier

Other children's titles by K. S. Brooks:

Postcards from Mr. Pish (Volumes 1-4)
Mr. Pish's Woodland Adventure
Mr. Pish Goes to the Farm
Mr. Pish's National Park Centennial Celebration
A Year with Mr. Pish (2013-Present)
Mr. Pish Calendar (2009-Present)

This Mr. Pish Backyard Adventure is a Brooks & Hise Production

ISBN-13: 978-1483931760
ISBN-10: 1483931765

CREDITS:

Pen & Ink Illustration by Gabriel Jules

This book is **dedicated** to all the ancient trees of the world, especially the Mighty Oak Tree in my backyard.

A Special Thanks to:

Arline Chase for her patience and support;
Gabriel Jules for her talented pen;
Stephen Hise for being the best writing partner ever;
and to Mr. Pish for making every project perfect.

My name is Mr. Pish. I'm a Jack Russell Terrier with curly hair. I'm kind of famous. I've met mayors and Mounties and even been in parades!

Before I traveled all over North America, I lived in Maryland, near the Chesapeake Bay. And guess what? I had the biggest oak tree in the neighborhood right in my yard. Honest! I'm not kidding.

I am pleased to introduce you to the Mighty Oak.

Just look at the size of that tree! It's ginormous! Okay, that's not a real word, but it mixes giant and enormous together to make ginormous! Have you ever seen a tree this big? Look at how much taller it is than the house.

I've never really wanted to climb a tree before (other than to catch a squirrel), but I think it would be awesome to climb this one. I wonder how far I could see.

What street do you think the tree lives on?
Can you guess the name?

2

I think someone saw the Mighty Oak Tree many years ago and thought it was so beautiful they named the street after it. Don't you?

How do I get a street named after me???

The tree doctor says the Mighty Oak Tree is three hundred years old. Don't you think that's really old? That means this tree was born before the Revolutionary War!

People still rode horses instead of driving cars, and they used candles instead of lamps, because electricity wasn't invented yet!

Can you think of anything else that old?

The Mighty Oak Tree has many jobs.

Can you guess what some of them are?

It doesn't need a briefcase or a computer.

It doesn't have to get in a car to go to work.

Although, I really do like going for rides in the car even though my humans won't let me drive. Shhhh.

In the Summer, the Mighty Oak Tree makes a lot of shade. Birds, animals, and people can go under it to stay cool when the sun is very hot.

I like resting in the shade on a hot day. Don't you?

It also gives animals a place to live.
Mr. and Mrs. Robin built this nest so they could make a family.

Their baby robins will stay here until they are old enough to fly on their own.

If you're quiet, you can hear the baby robins peeping for food!

A baby bird came
out of this egg.

Do you know
what kind?

That's a Robin's egg,
but don't tell anyone I
told you that!

Did you know that squirrels build nests too?

They get leaves and big branches from the Mighty Oak
Tree to build their house.

7

This Great Blue Heron came to the Mighty Oak on a cloudy day to get some wood to build her nest.

She broke a big stick off the Mighty Oak Tree, and then flew to her new home with it.

Lots of different animals use the Mighty Oak to build their houses.

Meet Mr. Snake.

He eats bugs and spiders and keeps the inside of the tree clean.

Even honey bees like to live on the Mighty Oak Tree.

They made their house here, out of wax.

Sometimes when a tree is very, very big, seeds from other trees will land on it and start to grow.

Can you see how this little tree is growing really high up on the Mighty Oak?

So the Mighty Oak Tree is like an animal apartment building, a lumber store, and a parasol.

Do you think it has more jobs?

Yes!

The Mighty Oak Tree is also like a grocery store! In the Fall, it makes acorns. Squirrels love to eat acorns. Squirrels hide acorns in the ground so they can find them later during the winter and eat them. If you were a squirrel, could you remember where you buried all your acorns?

Lots of bugs come to very big trees. Squirrels and birds will also come to the Mighty Oak Tree to eat the bugs. This woodpecker likes to eat the ants that climb up the tree.

Can you believe they eat bugs? Yuck!

Do you know what this branch is?

It is part of a highway system! Squirrels use all the branches, up and down, and sideways, to get where they need to go.

Have you ever seen squirrels running and jumping from tree to tree?

Highways for people have rest areas. Sometimes birds and dragonflies and other animals who are traveling will stop at the Mighty Oak Tree to rest.

Did you ever stop at a rest area to get something to drink and stretch your legs?

This woodpecker stopped to clean his feathers.

Sometimes the Mighty Oak Tree is a playground, too.
Squirrels play hide and seek, and tag, and even
wrestle and race.

Do you think they think the Mighty Oak Tree is their
jungle gym?

Even the leaves of the Mighty Oak Tree have a job. They breathe in carbon dioxide and send out oxygen so we can have cleaner air. That's a very important job, isn't it? I love clean air!

The Mighty Oak Tree is also a mommy and a daddy tree. Every year, it makes hundreds of acorns.

The squirrels eat many of them, but miss some, and lose some. Those acorns turn into baby trees!

There is a baby of the Mighty Oak Tree in the picture to the right. Can you find it?

Can you believe the Mighty Oak Tree was that small once?
Do you think this baby will get as big some day?

These other trees in my yard could be very grown up
children of the Mighty Oak Tree. They are big and tall, but
not as old.

I have the best yard, don't you think?

Do you know what the different parts of a tree are?

The roots are the part of the tree that grows in the ground. The roots drink water and get good vitamins from the dirt to keep the tree healthy.

Roots can go very far and very deep looking for the right food for the tree.

Doesn't this root look like an elephant's face?

16

These roots come up all over the yard and go back under ground. The roots hold the tree in the ground. If a very strong wind blows the tree, healthy roots will stop the tree from falling over.

The trunk is the first part of the tree that comes out of the ground.

The trunk of the Mighty Oak Tree is more than sixteen feet around!

Do you think you could reach around the trunk and touch your hands together? Not by yourself! It is so big that it would take four or more grown-ups to reach around it!

The lowest branches come out of the Mighty Oak Tree more than twelve feet above the ground!

How tall are you? Do you think you could you reach that lowest branch? Not even the world's tallest person can!

The trunk and branches are covered in bark. Bark is like the skin of the tree.

Vitamins and other important nutrients are carried to every part of the tree by the inside of the bark.

Just like your skin, bark can get boo-boos. Bark will try to grow back. Look at this smoother, rounded area. That is where the bark is healing.

Can you tell the difference?

Did someone really just say bark? Ha! That's dog humor. Get it?

The branches of the Mighty Oak Tree reach very far and very high to get lots of sun.

The leaves of the tree absorb vitamins from the sun light.

Do you think that's a lot of leaves?

The leaves make food that goes to the sap in the very inner layer of the bark. Sap is like the blood of the tree.

The sap takes all the food from the leaves and the roots and moves it around the tree to keep it healthy.

In the fall, when there is less sun because the days are shorter, the leaves of the Mighty Oak Tree turn gold and yellow and brown and fall to the ground.

In the forest, fallen leaves insulate and enrich the soil. Wow, trees are helpful!

In the Spring, the tree will make lots of little flowers that look like green beards.

When they fall off, new leaves will grow all over again.

At night, the Mighty Oak Tree can see every star in the sky.

I bet there are owls and bats and other nocturnal animals which visit the Mighty Oak at night. I wish I could see them.

They have an awesome view of the moon and all the planets because the tree is so tall that nothing else blocks it.

Would you like to be that tall?

I think I would.

Nocturnal means that they are active at night. Cool, huh?

22

Now you know all the important jobs of the Mighty Oak.

I feel very special living in the same yard
as that huge, old tree. Wouldn't you?

That's the end, get it? Ha! Dog humor again!

The End

Thank you very much for purchasing **The Mighty Oak and Me.** We hope that you had fun and learned some things at the same time.

Here's a fun worksheet for you. My secretary had some very nice teachers review it (and all my books, too) to make sure it was good for kids and would help them learn in a fun and interactive way. If you would like to download this worksheet, you can do it for free at my website, www.MrPish.com

If you enjoyed this book, please make sure to tell your friends. We would also appreciate it if you would leave a review so other people can know what you thought.

All Mr. Pish books and apps are geared towards outdoor learning and literacy. We hope you will check them out.

If you'd like, you can sign up for my newsletter on my website so you can learn about new releases, contests, and free books.

Okay, have fun with the worksheet! The answers are on the back page. Woof!

The Mighty Oak and Me

Learning is Fun! Worksheet

1. How old is the Mighty Oak tree?

   _____

2. What are the different parts of the Mighty Oak Tree?
   - a) Bark
   - b) Trunk
   - c) Tail
   - d) Acorn

3. What is like the blood of the Mighty Oak Tree?
   - a) Maple Syrup
   - b) Bark
   - c) Roots
   - d) Sap

4. Can you list some of the animals that visited the Mighty Oak Tree? (hint: see pages 5, 6, 8, and 9)

   _____

5. What does the Mighty Oak Tree provide so animals can build their nests?
   - a) Sticks
   - b) Leaves
   - c) Acorns
   - d) Branches

6. The Mighty Oak makes which of the following things?
   - a) Acorns
   - b) Leaves
   - c) Flowers like Green Beards
   - d) French Toast

7. Which job below is not a job for the Mighty Oak Tree?
   - a) Grocery Store for Animals
   - b) Race Car Driver
   - c) Rest Area
   - d) Shade

8. What color do the Mighty Oak's leaves turn in the Fall?
    a) Purple
    b) Green
    c) Yellow
    d) White

9. Would you want to rake all the leaves that fall to the ground each year?

10. You can color this picture!

11. Where can you go to find a Big Tree near where you live?

_____

12. Who do you think might live in or visit a Big Tree near you?

_____

13. What special fun could you have in your Big Tree?

_____

14. Why do you think it is really important for your city, your state, and the world to have lots of trees?

_____

_____

15. Draw a picture of yourself with your favorite Big Tree!

I hope you enjoyed the worksheet. Here are the answers:

1: 300 years old
2: a, b, d
3: d
4: Squirrels, robins, great blue herons, snakes, woodpeckers, bees, and more!
5: a, b, d
6: a, b, c
7: b
8: c
14: Clean air, places for animals to live...

Don't forget, you can visit me any time at the following places on the internet:
Website: www.MrPish.com
Facebook: Facebook.com/MrPish
Twitter: @MisterPish
Instagram: Instagram.com/MrPish
Amazon: http://amzn.to/2bl7gVd

Thank you again!

They said "bark." I still think that's funny! Ha!